GEORGIA DUSK

GEORGIA DUSK
where we were born

DUDGRICK BEVINS

LUKE KURTIS

bd nyc

Georgia Dusk: Where We Were Born

Published by bd-studios.com in New York City, 2017
Copyright © 2017 by Dudgrick Bevins & luke kurtis

Cover photo and photos on pages 28–43 and 60 by Dudgrick Bevins. Title page photo and photos on pages 8–25 and 44–59 by luke kurtis.

Design and Photo Sequence by luke kurtis

ISBN 978-0-9992078-2-6

All Rights Reserved. No part of this publication may be reproduced, stored in a retrieval system or transmitted in any form or by any means without the prior permission in writing of copyright holders and of the publisher.

Sometimes a wind in the Georgia dusk
Scatters hate like seed
To sprout its bitter barriers
Where the sunsets bleed.

        —Langston Hughes
         from "Georgia Dusk"

CONTENTS

THE LAST HAPPY DAYS
by LUKE KURTIS — 9

(T)HERE AND T/HERE
by DUDGRICK BEVINS — 29

BETWEEN HERE AND THERE
by LUKE KURTIS — 45

ABOUT THE POEMS AND PHOTOS — 61

THE LAST HAPPY DAYS

by LUKE KURTIS

there was a time
when things were simple
days were happy
and i sat up in my room
looking down at the back porch
out across the fields
wondering what my life
would be like
in years to come

i was to follow
in my sister's steps
—school in Atlanta—
everything was ready
the acceptance set
i would move in at Georgia State
and make it my home
for at least a few years

but things didn't happen that way

the farm is a relic
a ruin
a bucket full of dirty water
tears caught
welling up from the pain of this place
the pain of hate withered
toiling beneath the ground
pushing up from graves
like skeleton coffins
coming back to life

i've forgotten what it was like
to wake up in those chains

i've made amends by leaving
behind those last happy days
sinking into the earth

when i was a boy
my father bought a wooden hot tub
with planks held together by large rings
the wood would swell
joined by grooves
making a pool to rest the body

when dad put together this tub
he filled it with water
—cold—from the well
and i jumped inside
eager to swim

paddling about
soon coming out
chilled

the tub never worked well
and soon fell into disrepair
another relic
another ruin
to sit around
and become part of this place
the extended landscape
of tractors and machines
and other broken things
left to wither

years after i moved away
dad cut down the planks
and made the tub into a garden bed
where mother tends to flowers

"where did you plant flowers this spring?"
i asked my mother recently
"out there in the hot tub," she replied
and i could see in her eyes
the joy of growing plants
and taking old things
to make something new

i remember a plant in the house
with leaves green like watermelon stripes
and a single dead strand
hanging down the side
—sad, dry—
a part of life transformed
—dying—

i thought, "that is me"
i thought, "i see myself in that plant"
and so i continued:
"this is life"
"that plant is—everything—"
"that plant is god"

it seemed odd, as if something had taken hold
among the smothering haze of family
that there might be something more
than what tradition taught

once again i thought, "that plant is god"

i walked to the mailbox
collected a new issue of Rolling Stone
flipping through pages
of articles and interviews
—music, news—
all the things teenagers do
to find themselves

i spread out the magazines
across my bedroom floor
looking at the Calvin Klein men
and wanting more

like the time when my best friend
spent the night
and we wrestled on the bed
teenage horseplay teasing
my hand reaching for his crotch
—i didn't mean any harm—
he pulled away in a violent jerk
backing into my dresser
where an antique glass jug
—a relic i had dug up in the barn—
came crashing to the floor
in a waterfall of pennies and dimes

"you'd better not have grabbed me on purpose,"
he chimed, eyes sharp in defense
"i didn't mean to!" i whined

though i did not regret the attempt
for it was the closest i had ever been
to touching another man's cock

the jagged jug
like an eloquent blade
stayed on my dresser
until after i moved away
and my room became a relic
like the rest of the farm

i look back on those days
before the exile
and think about that place
how it is part of who i am
how—even then—i was looking deeper
how the fields and streams
—the plants, the trees—
—nature's temple—
taught me how and who to be

it was a time
when things were simple
days were happy
and i sat up in my room
looking down at the back porch
out across the fields
wondering what my life
would be like
in years to come

and here i have traveled far
leaving behind the last happy days

yet still i remember them

(T)HERE AND T/HERE

by DUDGRICK BEVINS

It starts with two ropes tied between two poplar trees / creating a gateway / a portal cutting through the veil I was only then learning to see / imagine me, eight years old with a dull-bladed hunting knife / a hand-me-down with a handle that smelled like car keys or pennies mixed with palm sweat / imagine me, taking off my clothes, folding each item neatly into a pile / black denim, a t shirt, shoes, and socks / I am nothing but underwear and fear / facing the ritual I've dreamed into being in order to see the last times of my memory.

The last time I was (t)here I buried my dead with uncalloused hands, glovelessly planting my grandfather like a spudding tuber in the Georgia land — nothing but unyielding red clay to cover him in his vault of decay. Where I'm from, we throw dirt on caskets with bare hands. Sometimes we cry and beg at the graveside.

Where I'm from the men carry the dead like a burden of honor, as if medals were awarded for pallbearing. We are a people so eager for another life, yet fearful of the possibilities of our own torch lights.

> *I touch the spell / my palm again the invisible wall of air / and seeing my last time of the other side, I recoil / the ripples of my fingerprints cling there / the grooves of my identity, the same as waves / and I'm cold / shivering in skivvies / shaking my blade / what is there for me to find on the other side of time / I see, also, the first time.*

I was born an explorer: an earthship astronaut ready to take on the world, and at three I took off walking, marching with my little legs, in hopes of finding something new. Perhaps to find the elves and trolls I knew were hiding in the leafy branches and the hollowed stumps and in the tangled briar of blackberry and muscadine — I knew new life was waiting just outside the porch and the dirt road and the mailbox and the driveway. Somewhere in the woods, I'd find another way. But instead, at three, I'm crying. Lost. Lonely. Fearful. I'm waiting, drenched in tears, for my father to save me from the towering trees — the pines that climb the ladder of the sky up so far it obscures heaven. And black limbs against blue, against cotton clouds, I'm in the arms of safety — of my father — and I'm home again, and in that home for the last time.

I'm blown back / dirtying the white cotton seat of my ass / it's all bone and alabaster flesh mixing hard into the dead leaf loam / this, the gift of my portal of rope and tree, showing me more than I had bargained for / somehow me, the history of my weakness / the history of my need / safety and passion mixing with the urge to leave / imagine me again, dusting off my ass and checking the rope for tautness and stability / I pluck it like catgut string / thinking back to another rope and another escape attempt.

Once, at maybe six or seven, I wanted to fly and took my father's old ratty ropes and made a spiderweb in my jungle gym. I thought, not even knowing the word, that if I could find my center of gravity and tie a rope there, I'd balance in midair. I knew in the logic of my childhood that my top was heavier than my hips, so I looped one rope around my waist and another around my neck — then leapt into nothing with swift bare feet that couldn't feel the aluminum bar I'd stood on. And for a moment I dangled between summer blue sky and spring green grass, the sun, a warm friend greeting my back — until

the rope around my middle snapped and I hung instead by my chin, groping and gasping as the tallest of the blades tickled the tips of my big toes. Somehow I had the breath to yell so I yelled — my mother running down hill with the look of a Valkyrie, lifting me, and giving me breath for the last time.

> *These portals are made of wishing and memory — they go as far forward as they go back / once in high school / my face in sweat-stinking pillows / adolescent / ear buds and discman lulling me / I saw a future me — no ropes needed, and no trees / but this me / naked me / forest magic creature communing with the creeks / I collected one of each / maple leaf oak leaf / poplar blossom / a branch with twenty eight pine needles / and two sprigs of hemlock / because time magic is most powerful in evergreens / I wished to see and to be / and the portal between the trees opened for me.*

Packing boxes with as much dust as stuff — half the weight of every book I pack is memories, or at best just simply dirt. But I have to pack lightly. People in New York have so little — my adolescent vision didn't tell me that: it just whispered "New York" in my ear and showed me walking, the omniscient view of god, a good head of hair and a mosaic marble compass inlayed on the street, me checking my wrist for the time, in a hurry to be some place. Ten years later, filling boxes, I wonder if I'll find such a space in my wanderings of the new place.

> I arranged sigils in the river rock / a preparatory step / necessary for aligning time / one on the creek bank / another on the tiny island / and a last in the fork of two nameless waterways / I left myself a pebble breadcrumb trail back to my home / following the curves of the old logging road / in case I wanted to go back / but I'd rather look forward.

It is the last night I will sleep in my parent's house, as my parent's child, in the bed of my youth. It is the last night I will close my eyes under this roof. It is my last summer of dragonflies and tiger lilies and elephant ears and lightening bugs, my last summer of sweet tea and kudzu and mountains the shape of children playing under green-brown braided rugs. The last time I see every quarry cave and pig farm, every hay barn and baptist church, every apple tree and rain-muddied river as somehow mine.

> *A reflection appears / a final image / another version of myself / equally naked / equally vulnerable / however, I'm grown / a man / hair on my knuckles and shoulder blades / staring back through the portal / his movements mimic my own / a perfect mirror / his right hand following my left only two feet taller / tracing something invisible / his ropes are tied between the alley walls / between two buildings / his background, one of bricks, not trees / his feet on trash and cement, not dead leaves / and me here me now presses my palm against that of me then me there / everything is one thing / I am as much here as I am there.*

BETWEEN HERE AND THERE
by LUKE KURTIS

i have tough feet
from growing up in the country
climbing trees
winding down gravel roads barefoot
and walking to the creek

after i moved to New York
i walked down Christopher Street
to hang out at the piers
jutting into the Hudson
a place where queers
met for sex and sunning

it was an in-between time
before the river park
filled with bikes and rollerblades
it was the glory days
when the city was new
and my heart leapt
watching sunset over Jersey

New York sunsets are worthy
and of special note
where reflections bounce
off glass towers
like monolith stones
in memory of our ancestors
like the tombstones scattered
across the hills of my youth

we come from somewhere else
most all of us, Americans
country of immigrant dreamers
bankers, doctors, farmers, cleaners
the whole lot of us
exiles, expatriates, and slaves

my ancestors came across the sea
generations ago
and settled in an Appalachian valley
among Cherokee hills and old growth forests
planting fields of cotton
and sowing hay

the memory of red clay
caked between my toes
seems far removed
from city sidewalks i now tread
where i cannot even go down to the river
to wash my feet or
seek forgiveness and baptism

the Village is lined with brownstones
homes dating back over a century
holding memories and stories
like Georgia barns hide secrets
hanging in the loft
and country churches string them up
dangling from the steeple by a noose

the Marlton House was built in 1900
turn of the century SRO
where my poet comrades stayed
from Kerouac to Millay

pre-war apartment buildings
pile upon modern streets
the sculpture of Rock Center
the lounges of Radio City
this glory, this decadence
is the epitome of New York style
the excess of jazz and deco and bop

the Titanic sank in 1912
and her survivors were brought
to the Jane Hotel by the river

my grandmother was born in 1913
on the family plantation
in the Appalachian foothills

i can trace a thread
between here and there
from this isle of Manhattan
to that Georgian valley
for my life is in these places
and i am of them
equally

i ascend from the subway
pull the hood of my jacket
over my head
to protect against the wind
cracking the skin of my lips
hardened from the bleeding winter
tough skin from head to toe

when the sun sets behind
those darkened hills
where i walked barefoot through the trees
i will remember those long shadows
like the World Trade Center
towering over this island
as i look south down 6th Avenue
from Greenwich Village

and know i am home

ABOUT THE POEMS AND PHOTOS

The series of photos accompanying "the last happy days" were made by luke kurtis in 1997 on his family farm in Villanow, Georgia. They are among the artists first photographic works. The poem was inspired by the photos and was written in 2017 in New York City.

The photos from "(T)here and T/Here" (written 2017) were made by Dudgrick Bevins, mostly in 2007, with a Vivitar Ultra Wide and Slim camera. The photos with a blue color shift were shot on film molded in bread for two months; the red-shifted images were created by exposing the film base rather than emulsion. All other photos were taken with a Nikon N75 with FujiFilm.

kurtis wrote "between here and there" in response to Bevins's above text. The photos were made in recent years in New York City, except the final photo, which was captured on the artist's family farm in Villanow as part of his site-specific installation project *convergence*.

While the strange symmetries—1997 to 2007 to 2017—are all coincidental, it seems the old photos not only summoned new poems, but they were brought together in much the same way both artists were drawn to New York City.

other books by luke kurtis

Angkor Wat
The Language of History
INTERSECTION

other titles published by bd-studios.com

Tentative Armor by Michael Harren
Visions of the Beyond by Stefanie Masciandaro
Puertas Españolas by Josemaria Mejorada & May Gañán
Jordan's Journey by Jordan M. Scoggins
Just One More by Jonathan David Smyth
Retrospective by Michael Tice

www.ingramcontent.com/pod-product-compliance
Lightning Source LLC
Chambersburg PA
CBHW040330300426
44113CB00020B/2716